KNEELING AMONG LIONS

PRAYING WHEN YOUR CHILD HAS A MENTAL ILLNESS

KIRSTEN PANACHYDA

INTRODUCTION

In *Among Lions: Fighting for Faith and Finding Your Rest while Parenting a Child with Mental Illness*, I describe this experience:

> When a child suffers, the parents enter into the place of pain too. Beasts encircle us. Drawn by our vulnerability, these enemies gather, ready to prey on our souls. Creatures we may have had only passing acquaintance with before become all too real and terrifying. We cannot escape. We may have some defenses, but not weapons that will destroy them utterly. We cannot drive the beasts away.
>
> We must live there, among them. If we are parenting a child with mental illness, we are there for the long haul. Throwing ourselves against the walls of our circumstances will only leave us exhausted, bruised, and hopeless. For our faith to survive, we must learn to fight the beasts in an arena we did not choose. Our souls, precious in the sight of God, deserve guarding. If we are to find rest, then it needs to be right there in the middle of the beasts.
>
> And God meets us there — in that inescapable place of grief, and pain, and fragility. There He proves again that He is a God full of lovingkindness, faithful to deliver.

This companion devotional is designed to help parents bring their aching hearts to God as they dwell among lions. You could use it for four weeks, five days per week. If you choose this schedule, you will find each week has a devotion each for issues of pain, fatigue, fear, and sense of self, as well as a psalm. However, the devotions do not need to be done every day, or in any particular order. This is a guide to praying for yourself — for your own soul, precious to God. A vibrant inner life with peace and strength is possible, even with the pain in your parenting journey.

> *Be gracious to me, O God, be gracious to me,*
> *For my soul takes refuge in You;*
> *And in the shadow of Your wings I will take refuge*
> *Until destruction passes by.*
> *I will cry to God Most High,*
> *To God who accomplishes all things for me.*
> *He will send from heaven and save me;*
> *He reproaches him who tramples upon me. Selah.*
> *God will send forth His lovingkindness and His truth.*
> *My soul is among lions;*
> *I must lie among those who breathe forth fire,*
> *Even the sons of men, whose teeth are spears and arrows*
> *And their tongue a sharp sword.*
> *Psalm 57:1-4*

I pray that as you use this guide, you will draw close to God Most High, our refuge, who accomplishes all things for us.

1

PEOPLE DON'T UNDERSTAND

"Boy, those teenage years can be tough, can't they?"

"Heh, heh, heh. Mark Twain said, 'When a child turns 12, he should be kept in a barrel and fed through a hole, until he reaches 16...at which time you should plug the hole.'"

"Kids are so over-medicated these days."

"Just let them know the consequences and then be consistent."

"Every teen has mood swings. It's the hormones."

"Siblings always fight."

"Boys will be boys."

"Girls are like that."

People. Don't. Understand.

GOD, it strikes at my heart when other people don't understand what I'm going through with my child. Ignorant or dismissive comments hurt. When I try to explain, judgmental stares and blank looks increase my pain.

You have known every kind of parenting grief. Your first children, Adam and Eve, made self-destructive choices. Moses believed lies about himself, arguing with God about his inabilities. Saul, the first king You gave Israel, was violent and unstable. Jacob, a carrier of Your promises, proved deceptive and manipulative. Your great prophet Elijah experienced suicidal thoughts.

You are the One who understands. You see into my heart and my days.

Would You treat these wounds, Great Healer?

Help me forgive, knowing I didn't really understand either before it was my kid.

Help me know when to advocate and when to let it go. Give me wise words when it's time to speak, and peace when it's not.

Let me find comfort in Your deep knowledge of my heart.

Amen

> *In the same way the Spirit also helps our weakness; for we do not know how to pray as we should, but the Spirit Himself intercedes for us with groanings too deep for words; and He who searches the hearts knows what the mind of the Spirit is, because He intercedes for the saints according to the will of God.*
> *Romans 8:26-27*

Adam and Eve: Genesis 3
Moses: Exodus 3 and 4
Saul: I Samuel 20
Jacob: Genesis 27
Elijah: I Kings 19

WHAT HAVE people said to me that showed lack of understanding? How did I respond?

-
-
-
-
-

GOD, help me forgive:

-
-
-
-
-

WISE WORDS FOR NEXT TIME:

-
-
-
-
-

2

MY COURAGE IS USED UP

The book of Exodus tells the story of how God used Moses, a disgraced prince turned shepherd, to deliver the nation of Israel from slavery in Egypt. When Moses first hears God's call to free his people, he is less than enthusiastic. He doesn't want to go. He feels unqualified. He doesn't think anyone will listen to him or believe him. Finally, assured of God's presence, though still unsure of himself, he goes. He appears before the ruler of Egypt. He demands that Pharaoh let the Israelites go.

And...

It doesn't work.

Pharaoh not only refuses, but he gets angry and oppresses the Israelites even more. The people are completely disappointed and mad at Moses.

"Then Moses returned to the LORD and said, "O Lord, why have You brought harm to this people? Why did You ever send me? Ever since I came to Pharaoh to speak in Your name, he has done harm to this people, and You have not delivered Your people at all."" (Exodus 5:22-23)

It must have felt like betrayal and abandonment to him. He thought he had done his big, brave thing and failed miserably. He thought all his courage and resolve had been poured out and wasted.

GOD, I feel like this. I cannot imagine ever being able to exercise more fortitude than I've already exercised, or overcoming more mental and emotional resistance. I feel just like I imagine Moses felt — that things are going from bad to worse and I have already used up every ounce of inner strength.

But God, it wasn't true for Moses. Today, I can look ahead in my Bible and see there are a bunch of chapters left in the story. Moses's acts of courage, the wonders of God, and the miraculous deliverance had not even really begun.

I want to trust there is more to my story too. I will believe that You can keep deepening the well of bravery inside me. I will trust that the drilling down for more courage will tap into a spring of water welling up from divine love.

I know You will be with me even through a long, arduous journey. I know You will show up if I'm stuck between an army and an impassable sea. Please give me the courage and strength I need to do the next hard thing. Heal me with Your tenderness and love when my heart is broken. Provide patience and endurance when I am depleted.

Amen

> *But Moses said to the people, "Do not fear! Stand by and see the salvation of the Lord, which He will perform for you today; for the Egyptians whom you have seen today, you will never see them again, ever. The Lord will fight for you, while you keep silent.*
> *Exodus 14:13-14*
>
> *The Lord is my strength and song,*
> *And He has become my salvation;*

This is my God, and I will praise Him;
My father's God, and I will exalt Him.
The Lord is a warrior;
The Lord is His name.
Exodus 15:2-3

WHAT WAS a situation when I had to be brave?

-
-
-
-
-
-
-

What is something I am afraid I will not be able to handle?

-
-
-
-
-
-

A short prayer asking God to help me trust:

-
-
-
-
-
-

3

PARENT RADAR

Years of tuning in to the emotions and subtleties of our kids develop a Parent Radar. Crisis heightens and hones this intuition. Adding the difficulties of parenting a child with mental illness may bias the radar toward hyper-sensitivity/suspicion. It is that exquisitely uncomfortable sense that something is not right, more is happening than meets the eye, or deception is taking place.

GOD, sometimes I really hate it.

OF COURSE, Parent Radar helps protect my kids when they need a parent to step in. But as they grow older, their choices are more their own. So are the consequences — this thought terrifies me. The clanging alarms of Parent Radar can't often alert me to danger I can circumvent anymore. Instead, they prompt me to have yet another conversation advising caution, common sense, wisdom.

GOD, I really hate that.

. . .

GOD, would you help me practice holy detachment? I need to have a healthy emotional life apart from the unhealthy or harmful behaviors of my beloved child. I need that health to extend into the realm of my spirit. I want to practice the unconditional love of God. I want to parent well, centered in an eternal perspective, where the core of my life is in God alone. I want to trustingly surrender the ones I love to the wisdom and power of God.

The problem is, sometimes it feels safer to cling to the worry. Detaching can feel like a step out into the cold unknown. Worry deceives me into investing in its false real estate by telling me I get something out of it — control.

Accepting my complete lack of control scares me. Will I be without shelter when the storm intensifies?

God, remind me that when I practice holy detachment, I am running to the only real safety: Your strong arms.

Amen

> *I will lift up my eyes to the mountains; From where shall my help come? My help comes from the LORD, Who made heaven and earth. He will not allow your foot to slip; He who keeps you will not slumber. Behold, He who keeps Israel Will neither slumber nor sleep. The LORD is your keeper; The LORD is your shade on your right hand. The sun will not smite you by day, Nor the moon by night. The LORD will protect you from all evil; He will keep your soul. The LORD will guard your going out and your coming in From this time forth and forever.*
> *Psalms 121:1-8*

> *Be anxious for nothing, but in everything by prayer and supplication with thanksgiving let your requests be made known to God. And the peace of God, which surpasses all*

comprehension, will guard your hearts and your minds in Christ Jesus.
Philippians 4:6-7

The name of the LORD is a strong tower; The righteous runs into it and is safe.
Proverbs 18:10

He who dwells in the shelter of the Most High Will abide in the shadow of the Almighty. I will say to the LORD, "My refuge and my fortress, My God, in whom I trust!"
Psalms 91:1-2

How can I protect my core identity while I parent?
-
-
-
-
-
-
-
-
-

How can I maintain my sense of self as a precious child of God?
-
-
-
-
-
-
-
-
-

4

I'M SO CONFUSED

Clinical Depression
    Depression with self-harm
    Depression with suicidal ideation
Depression with psychotic features
Major Depressive Disorder
Major Depressive Disorder with disordered eating
Major Depressive Disorder with Borderline Personality features
Bipolar Disorder II

These are just some of the "official" diagnoses that have shown up on the paperwork for the same child over the years. In psychiatric diagnosis, fluidity is more often the norm than certainty, especially for adolescents. If there is a list of ten diagnostic features, and a child has five of them, instead of seven... well, do they have that or not? And so many symptoms, like hearing voices, or disordered eating, cross categories. Is it schizo-affective disorder or depression? OCD or Borderline Personality?

How about medications? There are so many psych meds, and hitting on the right one is often a system of trial and error. And then there are combinations and dosages, and the possibilities become endless. Each possibility has its own host of side effects.

Finding therapists, managing to get an appointment with a doctor, researching treatment facilities, plugging into outpatient programs...

And how do we pay for the care our kids need? Even if we have great insurance, it's still complicated. If the insurance isn't adequate, the process is opaque and frustrating at best, and heartbreaking at worst.

GOD, I am battling against a paralysis of confusion. It's easy to feel overwhelmed and incompetent. Help me remember I'm not alone, that other parents also experience bafflement when navigating mental illness and its treatment.

Lead me to good, reputable resources. Please help me sort out helpful recommendations from those that won't help.

Give me wisdom and clarity when finding mental health professionals and making treatment choices for my child. I know You care about the particulars of our situation.

Bring me people who will support me in prayer for wisdom and decision-making.

Amen

> *But if any of you lacks wisdom, let him ask of God, who gives*
> *to all generously and without reproach, and it will be*
> *given to him.*
> *James 1:5*

> *For You are my rock and my fortress; For Your name's sake*
> *You will lead me and guide me.*
> *Psalms 31:3*

> *I will instruct you and teach you in the way which you*
> *should go; I will counsel you with My eye upon you.*
> *Psalms 32:8*

*Your ears will hear a word behind you, "This is the way, walk
    in it," whenever you turn to the right or to the left.*
Isaiah 30:21

*But the Helper, the Holy Spirit, whom the Father will send in
    My name, He will teach you all things, and bring to your
    remembrance all that I said to you.*
John 14:26

THINGS I NEED to learn or decisions I need to make:

-
-
-
-
-
-
-

People who can pray for me:

-
-
-
-
-
-
-

Resources I can research:

-
-
-
-
-
-
-

A PSALM ABOUT PAIN

Psalm 31
In You, Lord, I have taken refuge;
Let me never be put to shame;
In Your righteousness rescue me.

2
Incline Your ear to me, rescue me quickly;
Be a rock of strength for me,
A stronghold to save me.

3
For You are my rock and my fortress;
For the sake of Your name You will lead me and guide me.

4
You will pull me out of the net which they have secretly laid for me,
For You are my strength.

5
Into Your hand I entrust my spirit;
You have redeemed me, Lord, God of truth.

6
I hate those who devote themselves to worthless idols,
But I trust in the Lord.

7

I will rejoice and be glad in Your faithfulness,

Because You have seen my misery;

You have known the troubles of my soul,

8

And You have not handed me over to the enemy;

You have set my feet in a large place.

9

Be gracious to me, Lord, for I am in distress;

My eye is wasted away from grief, my soul and my body *too*.

10

For my life is spent with sorrow

And my years with sighing;

My strength has failed because of my guilt,

And my body has wasted away.

11

Because of all my adversaries, I have become a disgrace,

Especially to my neighbors,

And an object of dread to my acquaintances;

Those who see me in the street flee from me.

12

I am forgotten like a dead person, out of mind;

I am like a broken vessel.

13

For I have heard the slander of many,

Terror is on every side;

While they took counsel together against me,

They schemed to take away my life.

14

But as for me, I trust in You, Lord,

I say, "You are my God."

15

My times are in Your hand;

Rescue me from the hand of my enemies and from those who persecute me.

16

Make Your face shine upon Your servant;
Save me in Your faithfulness.

17

Let me not be put to shame, Lord, for I call upon You;
Let the wicked be put to shame, let them be silent in Sheol.

18

Let the lying lips be speechless,
Which speak arrogantly against the righteous
With pride and contempt.

19

How great is Your goodness,
Which You have stored up for those who fear You,
Which You have performed for those who take refuge in You,
Before the sons of mankind!

20

You hide them in the secret place of Your presence from the
conspiracies of mankind;
You keep them secretly in a shelter from the strife of tongues.

21

Blessed be the Lord,
For He has shown His marvelous faithfulness to me in a besieged
city.

22

As for me, I said in my alarm,
"I am cut off from Your eyes";
Nevertheless You heard the sound of my pleadings
When I called to You for help.

23

Love the Lord, all His godly ones!
The Lord watches over the faithful
But fully repays the one who acts arrogantly.

24

Be strong and let your heart take courage,
All you who wait for the Lord.

READ PSALM 31.

Compose your own similar psalm, using these prompts as a guide.
Declare that God protects and rescues:

-
-
-
-
-
-
-
-

Affirm your trust in God's goodness and care:

-
-
-
-
-
-
-
-

Lay out your distress, grief, and sorrows:

-
-
-
-
-
-
-

PROCLAIM GOD'S PAST FAITHFULNESS:

-

-

-

-

-

-

-

Confirm your trust in God:

-

-

-

-

-

-

-

I'M SO LONELY

God, I am so lonely sometimes.

Caring for my child makes me busier than ever. Finding time to connect with others seems impossible. Sometimes my child can't be left alone. It's hard to disappear from my life for weeks at a time because of a crisis.

If I keep declining invitations, they slow to a trickle and dry up. It's disheartening to be going through a painful parenting journey and also have to be the one who keeps up communication with friends. It may be natural, but it can also leave me feeling unloved.

Forgotten.

Lonely.

Sometimes, the illness can be so disruptive that I don't want to have anyone over to my own home either. Even family gatherings are fraught with chaos.

Posts and pictures on social media of other people's "normal" lives leave me feeling like I'm locked inside, looking out into a world passing me by. The loneliness stifles me.

Would You please help me find some relief? Lead me to a ministry or support group of people who understand. Give me courage to ask my friends to keep reaching out to me. Guard me from hurt when people let me down.

God, I know You are the Lover of my soul. You are always with me. Please comfort me in my loneliness.

Amen

> *God is our refuge and strength, a very present help in trouble.*
> *Psalm 46:1*

> *Where can I go from Your Spirit? Or where can I flee from Your presence? If I ascend to heaven, You are there; If I make my bed in Sheol, behold, You are there. If I take the wings of the dawn, if I dwell in the remotest part of the sea, even there Your hand will lead me, and Your right hand will lay hold of me.*
> *Psalms 139:7-10*

> *For I am convinced that neither death, nor life, nor angels, nor principalities, nor things present, nor things to come, nor powers, nor height, nor depth, nor any other created thing, will be able to separate us from the love of God, which is in Christ Jesus our Lord.*
> *Romans 8:38-39*

SLICES OF TIME in my week when I could connect with someone:

-
-
-
-
-
-
-

SAFE PEOPLE in my life I can call or email:

-
-
-
-
-
-
-

7

I FEEL LIKE I'M FAILING

I t's a common fantasy for stressed parents. To be by oneself with the car. Stopping at the bank and withdrawing the maximum amount. Going to the gas station and filling the tank. Popping into the grocery store and stocking up on nonperishables.

And then just taking off.

Disappearing.

Giving. Up.

GOD, it frightens me how appealing this fantasy is.

I've tried and tried, fought and fought, but I'm still losing the war. My kid's mental illness beats me at every turn. I feel so defeated.

How I wanted to do this parenting thing with and for You, God. And ever so subtly, I swallowed the idea that if I did everything right and tried hard, I would win at the parenting game.

But then came depression, self-harm, hospitalizations, suicidal ideation, then attempts... How are people of faith supposed to parent a kid with mental illness? I don't even know what winning looked like anymore, but I sure know what defeat feels like.

God, change the definition. Teach me, deep down, that to You, winning at parenting means faithfulness, not a "successful" outcome. Mend my sore heart. Keep me walking, depending, and trusting in You. Faithfulness is victory.

Please help me enjoy small moments of joy or progress. But don't let me take the blame or let my peace be destroyed by setbacks. Remind me that lack of crisis is not victory. Faithfulness is victory. One step in front of the other.

I belong to the One who faithfully walked this earth, who had "success" with very few, and who now lives, making all this stuff work together for my good.

Faithfulness for the win.

Amen

> *Therefore if you have been raised with Christ [to a new life, sharing in His resurrection from the dead], keep seeking the things that are above, where Christ is, seated at the right hand of God. Set your mind and keep focused habitually on the things above [the heavenly things], not on things that are on the earth [which have only temporal value]. For you died [to this world], and your [new, real] life is hidden with Christ in God."*
> *Colossians 3:1-3 (Amplified Version)*

How do I tend to measure my success as a parent?

-
-
-
-
-
-

What are some small steps of progress or moments of joy I can celebrate?

-
-
-
-
-
-

How have I been a faithful parent?

-
-
-
-
-
-

8

THREE LITTLE DOTS

The texts that make the heart pound.

"I need to tell you something..."

What? What would I be told? Would it be a poor decision with painful consequences? Would it be a relapse?

"Don't look at my stuff!"

Or even the more healthy: "I need you to throw something away for me."

What was I going to find? A piece of glass and empty Band-Aid wrappers? Bloody sheets? Suicidal song lyrics? An upsetting YouTube video? Drugs?

Three little dots blinking on the screen, marking the wait for the rest of the message.

The message, when it continues, might be benign, boring, unexceptional.

Those three little dots though.

GOD, they drilled into my peace. One ambiguous text and I was right back there: stomach churning, hands shaking, breath gasping. My body has not forgotten the feel of crisis.

But.

It is not the same. You have been working in my soul. My body may still react with a rush of adrenaline, but my mind retains the healing transformation.

> *Though a host encamp against me, My heart will not fear;*
> *Though war arise against me, In spite of this I shall be*
>   *confident.*
> *One thing I have asked from the LORD, that I shall seek:*
> *That I may dwell in the house of the LORD all the days of my*
>   *life,*
> *To behold the beauty of the LORD And to meditate in His*
>   *temple.*
> *For in the day of trouble He will conceal me in His tabernacle;*
> *In the secret place of His tent He will hide me;*
> *He will lift me up on a rock.*
> *Psalms 27:3-5*

The lesson that stitches up the wounds in my heart, the wisdom that applies healing balm to the tender scars is this:

My life is in God Alone.

You are my One Thing.

In the end, the texts, the heart-pound, the three little dots can only drill down so far. The bedrock is too much for that puny tool.

God, I know it might not be over. Crisis may come again. But it won't be the same, because I am not the same. I am forever changed by how I have already experienced the love and healing of the Unchanging One.

Please, in those moments when I find myself "back there," help me ride out the reaction with a secure knowledge of Your love for me.

Amen

How DOES my body react to fear or dread?

-
-
-
-
-
-
-

WHAT TECHNIQUES, like controlling my breathing, reciting a memorized Scripture, or drinking some water or a cup of tea, best help me ride out a fear reaction?

-
-
-
-
-
-

9

A DIFFERENT APPROACH

A pproaching prayer with a creative practice can help us enter into the reality of God's presence. I sometimes use poetry or song lyrics to help me pray. I wrote a poem out of my pain based on Psalm 57 ("My soul is among lions; I must lie among those who breathe forth fire" Psalm 57:4a) that eventually became the theme for *Among Lions* and for this devotional:

> *Beat on the door,*
> *Fists purpled and skin split.*
>
> *Prowling, prowling all around me.*
> *Teeth bared, breath hot and smelling of blood*
> *And hunger.*
>
> *Locked door behind me,*
> *This is my soul place now,*
> *With slashing claws and fanged teeth nearby*
> *Promising pain.*

This is where I must lie down now.

Yellow eye slants toward me,
Speaks fear and failure;
Toss of the head is accusatory.

My cries slam back to my ears
From impenetrable ceiling.

Circle the room to find escape,
See written small and faint
By those here before me
Counsel on stone wall to flesh heart:
Lie down.

Lie down among the lions.
Find rest. Slumber here.
Deliverance is not through the door,
But here, right here.
Lie down, but not unto death
Unto life.

CHOOSE a creative practice for your prayer time. Make a picture, dance, arrange flowers, design or work on a craft, build something, plan a garden. Make your activity a meditation on the goodness of God.

A PSALM ABOUT FATIGUE

P salm 86
Incline Your ear, Lord, *and* answer me;
For I am afflicted and needy.

2

Protect my soul, for I am godly;
You my God, save Your servant who trusts in You.

3

Be gracious to me, Lord,
For I call upon You all day long.

4

Make the soul of Your servant joyful,
For to You, Lord, I lift up my soul.

5

For You, Lord, are good, and ready to forgive,
And abundant in mercy to all who call upon You.

6

Listen, Lord, to my prayer;
And give *Your* attention to the sound of my pleading!

7

On the day of my trouble I will call upon You,
For You will answer me.

8

There is no one like You among the gods, Lord,
Nor are there any works like Yours.

9

All nations whom You have made will come and worship before You, Lord,
And they will glorify Your name.

10

For You are great, and you do wondrous deeds;
You alone are God.

11

Teach me Your way, Lord;
I will walk in Your truth;
Unite my heart to fear Your name.

12

I will give thanks to You, Lord my God, with all my heart,
And I will glorify Your name forever.

13

For Your graciousness toward me is great,
And You have saved my soul from the depths of Sheol.

14

God, arrogant men have risen up against me,
And a gang of violent men have sought my life,
And they have not set You before them.

15

But You, Lord, are a compassionate and gracious God,
Slow to anger and abundant in mercy and truth.

16

Turn to me, and be gracious to me;
Grant Your strength to Your servant,
And save the son of Your maidservant.

17

Show me a sign of good,
That those who hate me may see *it* and be ashamed,
Because You, Lord, have helped me and comforted me.

READ PSALM 86.

Compose your own similar psalm, using these prompts to guide you.

ASK God to listen to you:
-
-
-
-
-
-
-

WHY WILL GOD LISTEN? (Love, compassion, goodness, etc.)
-
-
-
-
-
-
-

How DO you know God can answer and help? (Power, wisdom, faithfulness, etc.)

-
-
-
-
-
-
-

How HAS God proven Himself to you before?

-
-
-
-
-
-
-

WHAT DO you need from God?

-
-
-
-
-
-
-

How do you want to respond to God's goodness? (Thank Him, follow him, give Him praise, etc.)

-
-
-
-
-
-
-

BONKED ON THE HEAD

There it is. The deception, again. The hiding, the lying, the misleading — so often a part of relating to a loved one who struggles with mental illness. The broken trust, the processing, the rebuilding. Helping them have healthier coping skills and responses to distress. Being supportive, drawing loving and firm boundaries.

But God — what about the fact that I am down-deep hurt? What about that knife wound of betrayal? What about my anger and frustration?

As a caregiver and support system member, I'm supposed to recognize that the illness is the enemy, not the one I love. I'm not supposed to take it personally. I'm supposed to stay the course with kindness and good training. Especially when I'm the parent — I'm the one who needs to be mature and act like a grown-up.

BUT YOU KNOW WHAT, God? It does hurt. I do get angry.

For little kids, one of the hardest things to learn is that it is right to say sorry even if they hurt someone unintentionally. If they throw a ball that misses the mark and bonks someone in the head, they should apologize. An apology is not an admission of guilt in that circumstance, but a recognition of being the cause of someone else's pain.

My kid can cause a wound with behavior that is not aimed at me personally, that is not intended to inflict hurt. But I still have the wound.

God, what do I do with that?

I know every good answer starts with bringing it to Jesus. Talk about it with You.

And when I listen, I hear Your gentle but implacable command to forgive. Not just overlook. Not just excuse because of mental illness.

Forgive.

Recognize my child is the cause, even if he didn't mean to.

Reminding myself that my kid is not the enemy and to not take it personally might take some of the sting out. But only forgiveness cleans out the wound and allows for healing.

God, help me forgive.

Amen.

Forgive us our trespasses, even as we forgive those who
trespass against us.
Matthew 6:12

Be kind, one to another, tenderhearted, forgiving one another,
even as God in Christ has forgiven you."
Ephesians 4:32

Bear with each other and forgive one another if any of you
has a grievance against someone. Forgive as the Lord
forgave you.
Colossians 3:13

WHAT HURTS HAS my child caused me, intentionally or unintentionally, that I need to forgive?

-
-
-
-
-
-
-

MY PRAYER ASKING the Holy Spirit to help me forgive:

-
-
-
-
-
-
-

12

I'M EXHAUSTED

It may not be the sharpest pain, but it is the most persistent. Exhaustion. Burnout. Sometimes it's physical, sometimes emotional, and often both. I pay out energy in every direction. The extra appointments for my child squeezing my schedules. The toll of agonizing decisions. The energy spent trying to respond well to crisis and conflict and chaos. The loss of sleep to grief or worry. The neglect of healthy habits in favor of comfort food and escapist TV. And it all just seems to go on and on.

God, I can find advice about self-care anywhere. Maybe I can even manage to be pampered for a bit. But what I really need is a soul-deep knowledge of Your unlimited love and compassion for me and my child.

I need to know You know. You see me. Me — with my eyes red from weeping and sleeplessness, my stress headache, my hair in desperate need of a cut and style, my extra pounds, my shortened temper.

God, let me rest in Your love.

And please, will You help me get the physical and emotional rest I need? Help me see and seize those opportunities for rest and refreshment. If I read the self-care articles, show me one or two things to put into practice. Please lead me to people or organizations that can help. Make me bold to ask friends and family.

Remind me of Your design for me and make a way for me to nurture my soul. Give me a little space to read, do crafts, hike. Just a little of something I love.

God, please help me sleep, long enough and soundly enough. Help me relieve some of the stress with the food and movement that is good for my body and mental wellness.

But most of all, compassionate God, relieve my deep weariness by removing the loads I'm carrying that are not meant for me. Deal with the false guilt that tells me: "If you're tired, you must not have enough faith!"

Thank You Jesus for showing me the truth when You came to live among us. You became tired. You sought rest in lonely places, away from crowds. My Savior, You collapsed on the way to Calvary. You had perfect faith, and that cross You dropped was certainly the burden You were meant to carry.

Jesus, You offer me not a saccharine promise of an easy life, but the true sweetness of rest in You. You know I will be weary and burdened. But You promise that it all matters to You.

Amen

> *Come to Me, all who are weary and heavy-laden, and I will*
> *give you rest. Take My yoke upon you and learn from Me,*
> *for I am gentle and humble in heart, and YOU WILL*
> *FIND REST FOR YOUR SOULS. For My yoke is easy*
> *and My burden is light.*
> *Matthew 11:28-30*

WHAT THINGS ARE EXHAUSTING and burning me out?

-
-
-
-
-
-

WHAT ARE gentle steps I can realistically take to ease my stress?

-
-
-
-
-
-

WHAT BURDEN IS God leading me to lay down?

-
-
-
-
-

13

I DON'T KNOW WHAT TO DO

The warrior stands on the crest of a hill. Although already wounded and tired, she is committed to the cause and ready to rush to the defense of her people. On her left, sounds of mayhem fill the valley as her people are slowly pushed toward the raging river. To her right, her people losing the high ground as they are overrun by strength of the enemy.

Which way should she run? Which battle needs her most? Which strategy will win the war? Which decision will prove a disastrous mistake? Choosing is impossible, but not choosing is unthinkable.

GOD, I don't know what to do. In taking care of my child with mental illness, there are so many choices, and often all of them seem bad.

Do we go to the emergency department? Which one?

Do we try this medication, with these side effects? Or that one, with those?

Do I call the police?

Should we keep our child in school? Which school?

Sometimes I'm unsure of my own judgment. Am I thinking rationally? Can my instinct be trusted?

God, my heart aches when I have to make the hard choices with no guarantees. Feeling so helpless to succeed at the thing that matters most. Bearing the crushing weight of responsibility. Depending on a roll of the dice when the stakes are so high.

You know what I'm facing. Help me recognize that all the choices may have flaws and there might not be one that is the magic bullet. Assure me that it's okay to do the best I can and let the rest go. I believe that You will give me wisdom when I ask. I trust You to protect me and my child

If my choice yields difficult consequences, help me remember that the others probably had equal dangers and don't actually know what You protected me and your child from.

Thank You that I can come to Your throne every day, every hour, every minute if I have to. The way is always open and You always welcome me. You are wise and You are able. You love me and mine. I entrust myself to Your tender care.

Amen

> *Therefore let us draw near with confidence to the throne of grace, so that we may receive mercy and find grace to help in time of need.*
> *Hebrews 4:16*

WHAT CHOICES AM I facing as I support my child?
-
-
-
-
-
-
-

MY PRAYER FOR WISDOM:
-
-
-
-
-
-
-

14

A VIBRANT INNER LIFE

For a person who longs to face life courageously, with a soul that is whole, the ability to cultivate a vibrant inner life is crucial. The problem is thieves that press in on every side, stealing the time and breathing room necessary for soul growth. Distraction. Crisis. Tasks. The needs, wants, or demands of others. Weariness.

Sometimes the sneakiest thief of all is a secret doubt that soul wholeness is possible.

GOD, can You mend a soul as wounded as mine?

If I read Scripture passages every morning and write in a journal a little, will it make a difference? I'm not looking for a magic charm. But will You help me believe — to put it crudely — that this will work? That I really can live through pain and disappointment and grief with joy and peace by resting in You, God? By obeying You, and soaking in Your Word? God, I ask for confirmation — strengthen my faith.

God I believe You will come through. I trust You to heal my soul as I spend time with You.

You know that carving out time to spend with You is a challenge. Please help me set aside just a few minutes. Show me how to be creative and not wait for perfect moments. Remind me I can keep it simple.

When I have a few minutes to relax, let me remember to build some soul cultivation into my relaxation, and put those practices first.

God, I want an inner life connected to You. I trust You will do beautiful work in me as I spend time with You.

Tending my soul will keep fear at bay and prevent me from weakening in the face of difficult circumstances. The experience of Your love and power will nourish my inner person so I can be strong and brave.

God, I enter this time with You without expectations of myself. Thank You for letting me just rest in the quiet of Your presence.

Amen

> *One thing I have asked from the Lord, that I shall seek:*
> *That I may dwell in the house of the Lord all the days of my*
>   *life,*
> *To behold the beauty of the Lord*
> *And to meditate in His temple.*
> *For on the day of trouble He will conceal me in His*
>   *tabernacle;*
> *He will hide me in the secret place of His tent;*
> *He will lift me up on a rock.*
> *And now my head will be lifted up above my enemies*
>   *around me,*
> *And I will offer sacrifices in His tent with shouts of joy;*
> *I will sing, yes, I will sing praises to the Lord.*
> *Wait for the Lord;*
> *Be strong and let your heart take courage;*
> *Yes, wait for the Lord.*
> *Psalm 27:4-6,14*

WHEN CAN I fit in a few minutes to spend time with God?

-
-
-
-
-
-
-

WHAT SIMPLE PRACTICES can I try?

-
-
-
-
-
-

15

A PSALM ABOUT FEAR

Psalm 56
Be gracious to me, God, for a man has trampled upon me;
Fighting all day long he oppresses me.

2
My enemies have trampled upon me all day long,
For they are many who fight proudly against me.

3
When I am afraid,
I will put my trust in You.

4
In God, whose word I praise,
In God I have put my trust;
I shall not be afraid.
What can *mere* mortals do to me?

5
All day long they distort my words;
All their thoughts are against me for evil.

6
They attack, they lurk,
They watch my steps,

As they have waited *to take* my life.

7

Because of *their* wickedness, *will there be* an escape for them?
In anger make the peoples fall down, God!

8

You have taken account of my miseries;
Put my tears in Your bottle.
Are they not in Your book?

9

Then my enemies will turn back on the day when I call;
This I know, that God is for me.

10

In God, *whose* word I praise,
In the Lord, *whose* word I praise,

11

In God I have put my trust, I shall not be afraid.
What can mankind do to me?

12

Your vows are *binding* upon me, God;
I will render thanksgiving offerings to You.

13

For You have saved my soul from death,
Indeed my feet from stumbling,
So that I may walk before God
In the light of the living.

READ PSALM 56.

Compose your own similar psalm, using these prompts as a guide.

TELL GOD what you are afraid of:

-
-
-
-
-
-
-

HOW DOES YOUR FEAR FEEL?

-
-
-
-
-
-
-

DECLARE that you know God is on your side:

-
-
-
-
-
-
-

THANK God for paying attention and caring about your distress:

-
-
-
-
-
-
-

RECOUNT WHAT GOD has already done for you:

-
-
-
-
-
-
-

CONFIRM your trust that God will protect your soul:

-
-
-
-
-
-
-

16

SOWING SEEDS

The weeping time comes to all humans. It's all right to have that painful season. Going through days with an ache in the chest and leaking eyes — this is part of life. But what do I do with it, this period of grief and fragmentation?

OH GOD, during the weeping, let me sow seeds. Let me plant as an act of faith. I believe these shriveled, dry things, poked into soil, will transform. Faith accepts the weary task that muddies hands and feet. Faith in the God of resurrection assures me that the labor of grief, there in the dirt soaked by the saline that drips off my face, is valuable.

God, assure me that absence of weeping is not evidence of faith. Practicing faith during the weeping is what brings forth harvest.

In my greatest weeping time, I sometimes can't imagine a harvest of good, but God, in Your mercy, lead me to sow anyway. Let these seeds fall from my hand into that mud:

Jesus loves me, this I know.

This I know, that God is for me. (Psalm 56:9b)

Hope in Christ does not disappoint. (Romans 5:5)

Parched, misshapen little nuggets of faith, planted in rows made crooked by the fact that my eyes are clouded by tears. To me they don't look like they could become a field of harvest, but I believe in a God who made the world with His word and a Word Who makes heirs with His blood.

You bring the harvest to me.

I will always be held.

You will make all things new.

My life is hid with God in Christ.

Amen

> *Those who sow in tears shall reap with joyful shouting. (S)he who goes to and fro weeping, carrying (her) bag of seed, shall indeed come again with a shout of joy, bringing (her) sheaves with her.*
> *Psalm 126:5-6*

> *This I know, that God is for me.*
> *In God, whose word I praise,*
> *In the Lord, whose word I praise,*
> *In God I have put my trust. I shall not be afraid.*
> *Psalm 59:9b-11*

> *We celebrate in hope of the glory of God. And not only this, but we also celebrate in our tribulations, knowing that tribulation brings about perseverance; and perseverance, proven character; and proven character, hope; and hope does not disappoint, because the love of God has been poured out within our hearts through the Holy Spirit who was given to us.*
> *Romans 5:2b-5*

WHAT TRIGGERS the weeping time for me? Exhaustion? Angry, hurtful words and slammed doors? Chronic stress? The not-knowing? A wrenching loss?

-
-
-
-
-
-
-

WHAT SEEDS CAN I put in my sower's bag to plant during the weeping time?

-
-
-
-
-
-
-

17

WILL GOD REALLY PROVIDE?

G od told the Israelites He would feed them in the wilderness, day by day. He had rescued them from slavery, and He would provide food every morning. The first time, the children of Israel didn't believe it. They tried to stock up on what they thought they'd need. They must have been afraid as well as disgusted the next morning when instead of breakfast, they found slime and maggots. They had not trusted the next day's provision. They gathered extra and stashed it away for the next day, in case God didn't come through for them. He spent the next forty years teaching them to trust and obey.

Trying to live on yesterday's strength is like trying to live on yesterday's manna. We need to access God's power every day, for that day's struggle. Except, except...

There was one day of the week when the manna stayed fresh overnight: the rest day. Did that day make them afraid too? No new manna on the ground — what did it mean? What about when the extra was used up? Would there be more after the rest day?

Sometimes we also are given a rest day from the struggle with our kid's mental illness. Sometimes even a whole rest season comes our way. The storehouse of memory becomes the making of rejoicing, a party. The celebration requires that we believe, from the witness of our memory, that strength will be provided again when we need it.

GOD, when you give me rest from the struggle, help me trust You enough to enjoy it. Let me pull out the stash of strength You provided in the "working days" and feast on Your goodness.

Remind me of the litany from my memory storehouse that I rehearse when I start to fear that I can't make it through another crisis again:

- You sent people with encouragement, empathetic tears, or information at just the right times.
- You provided Scriptures and the presence of Holy Spirit.
- You have shown me that even the path through the valley of the shadow of death is holy ground, because my Shepherd is with me.

YOU ARE the same God who walked me through the past nightmares and You will walk me through anything coming in the future. Fresh manna will always appear until I am safe in the Promised Land.

God, when I am in the "working days" and so weary, remind me that I will find my manna for the day. Please give me a rest day soon.

When You do, help me to feast and enjoy Your goodness.

Amen

> *Moses said to them, "It is the bread the Lord has given you to*
> *eat. This is what the Lord has commanded: 'Everyone is to*
> *gather as much as they need. Take an omer for each*
> *person you have in your tent.'"*
> *The Israelites did as they were told; some gathered much,*

*some little. And when they measured it by the omer, the
one who gathered much did not have too much, and the
one who gathered little did not have too little. Everyone
had gathered just as much as they needed.*

*Then Moses said to them, "No one is to keep any of it until
morning."*

*However, some of them paid no attention to Moses; they kept
part of it until morning, but it was full of maggots and
began to smell. So Moses was angry with them.*

*Each morning everyone gathered as much as they needed,
and when the sun grew hot, it melted away. On the sixth
day, they gathered twice as much—two omers for each
person—and the leaders of the community came and
reported this to Moses.*

*He said to them, "This is what the Lord commanded:
'Tomorrow is to be a day of sabbath rest, a holy sabbath
to the Lord. So bake what you want to bake and boil what
you want to boil. Save whatever is left and keep it until
morning.'"*

*So they saved it until morning, as Moses commanded, and it
did not stink or get maggots in it.*

*"Eat it today," Moses said, "because today is a sabbath to the
Lord. You will not find any of it on the ground today. Six
days you are to gather it, but on the seventh day, the
Sabbath, there will not be any."*

*Nevertheless, some of the people went out on the seventh day
to gather it, but they found none.*

*Then the Lord said to Moses, "How long will you refuse to
keep my commands and my instructions? Bear in mind
that the Lord has given you the Sabbath; that is why on
the sixth day he gives you bread for two days. Everyone is
to stay where they are on the seventh day; no one is to go
out." So the people rested on the seventh day.*

Exodus 16:15-30

*My flesh and my heart may fail, but God is the strength of my
    heart and my portion forever.*
Psalm 73:26

WHAT WAYS HAS God provided strength to me in the past?

-
-
-
-
-
-
-

KEEP ADDING TO IT. Pull out this list when you are fearful about whether you can handle the future

I HAVE SO MANY WORRIES

Sometimes caring for a child with mental illness seems all-consuming. But the task doesn't use up all of us, or we wouldn't keep feeling other worries gnawing away at us too.

GOD, please protect my heart. You invite me to bring my list of worries to You. As I do, set Your peace like a band of fierce bodyguards around my soul.

God, when I experience brain fog at work, help me think clearly and perform solidly. Banish that mushy feeling in my mind making it hard to retrieve information, stay on task, form coherent sentences. Help me when worry for my kid invades my thoughts. When it comes, remind me to take a breath, then practice techniques to help me minimize it and return to focus. Protect the job I need to support my family.

God, please shore up our defenses around my marriage. It's no secret that marriages can crumble under the pressure of parenting a child who needs special care. Please reassure me that my most important earthly relationship is not doomed to fail. Help me see what's going on in my own heart. Work in me. Give me an eternal perspective, and compassion for my spouse. Crush any growing bitterness with truth and hope. Heal wounds in our marriage by helping me focus on following Jesus.

God, take care of my other kids. They are dealing with so many mixed emotions. They love their sibling who is ill, but also resent the attention and chaos the illness brings. They want to support their obviously distressed parents, but also want to hide from the situation. Their own real needs for love and care may be neglected or put on hold during a crisis, and they understand, but ... You know how I agonize over them. I miss the cuddle time, the one-on-one outings, the cheerful family dinners that aren't happening to make their lives full of parental love. How will being raised in less-than-ideal circumstances will affect them in the long-term? Please give me time with each of my kids. Help me speak love to them that they can understand and receive. Redeem any losses they experience. Remind me that You are their God too.

As I bring these and all my worries to You God, free me from their bondage. Thank you caring about all the things that concern me. Thank you for working for me. Thank you sheltering me with Your incredible, incomprehensible peace.

Amen

Do not be anxious about anything, but in everything by prayer and pleading with thanksgiving let your requests be made known to God. And the peace of God, which surpasses all comprehension, will guard your hearts and minds in Christ Jesus.
Philippians 4:6-7

WHAT ARE my worries and anxieties? (make a list)

-
-
-
-
-
-
-

AT GOD'S INVITATION, bring each worry to God.

-
-
-
-
-
-
-

THANK God for His care and work on your behalf:

-
-
-
-
-
-

19

DOES MY SUFFERING MATTER?

Everywhere we look, we see a world of people who are suffering. A whole generation of refugee children growing up displaced. Millions trapped in the nightmare of human trafficking. Mental illness rampant, misunderstood, and under-treated. Wars that last decades without any winners, but countless losers.

Has the suffering in the world increased? Or is it only that I am overloaded with information, and so much of it carries the weight of suffering? Perhaps all that knowledge we can now access, the heaviness of it, is a kind of suffering in itself.

GOD, I feel so lethargic with it sometimes, as though gravity pulls more strongly than it should under my footsteps, even while my shoulders rise up in tension to my ears.

And meanwhile, I have my private suffering. A child lost in the wilderness of depression or anxiety. My loneliness. Worry. Confusion and helplessness.

The gravity pull of suffering collapses my frame under the weight.

God, I know every person suffers. The question is: what do I do with it?

More than that, I count all things to be loss in view of the
surpassing value of knowing Christ Jesus my Lord, for
whom I have suffered the loss of all things, and count
them but rubbish so that I may gain Christ, and may be
found in Him... that I may know Him and the power of
His resurrection and the fellowship of His sufferings,
being conformed to His death; in order that I may attain
to the resurrection from the dead.
Philippians 3:8-11

GOD, I want to know the power of resurrection when I respond to suffering in my life. Help me recognize that not only the bad stuff, but the good stuff too, is nothing compared to knowing and being found in Christ.

Will you please transform my suffering to be in fellowship with His? Since resurrection comes after participation in death, help me be willing to suffer for the sake of others and die to my own comfort.

God, I have an existential horror of pointless suffering. Don't allow suffering to pull me down into despair. Rescue me. Instead, may suffering pull me to face-down worship of the crucified, living Christ. Let suffering join my heart to His in service and compassion. Bring me to the place where deep calls to deep and my soul changes and grows and refines.

Amen

WHAT DO I find difficult to "count as rubbish" compared to knowing Christ? What dreams am I tempted to hold dearer than this?

-
-
-
-
-
-
-

WHAT AM I suffering from right now that I can ask God to transform for me?

-
-
-
-
-
-
-

A PSALM ABOUT WHO GOD IS AND WHO
I AM

P salm 103
    Bless the Lord, my soul,
    And all that is within me, *bless* His holy name.

2

Bless the Lord, my soul,
And do not forget any of His benefits;

3

Who pardons all your guilt,
Who heals all your diseases;

4

Who redeems your life from the pit,
Who crowns you with favor and compassion;

5

Who satisfies your years with good things,
So that your youth is renewed like the eagle.

6

The Lord performs righteous deeds
And judgments for all who are oppressed.

7

He made known His ways to Moses,

His deeds to the sons of Israel.

8

The Lord is compassionate and gracious,
Slow to anger and abounding in mercy.

9

He will not always contend *with us,*
Nor will He keep *His anger* forever.

10

He has not dealt with us according to our sins,
Nor rewarded us according to our guilty deeds.

11

For as high as the heavens are above the earth,
So great is His mercy toward those who fear Him.

12

As far as the east is from the west,
So far has He removed our wrongdoings from us.

13

Just as a father has compassion on *his* children,
So the Lord has compassion on those who fear Him.

14

For He Himself knows our form;
He is mindful that we are *nothing but* dust.

15

As for man, his days are like grass;
Like a flower of the field, so he flourishes.

16

When the wind has passed over it, it is no more,
And its place no longer knows about it.

17

But the mercy of the Lord is from everlasting to everlasting for those who fear Him,
And His justice to the children's children,

18

To those who keep His covenant
And remember His precepts, *so as* to do them.

19
The Lord has established His throne in the heavens,
And His sovereignty rules over all.
20
Bless the Lord, you His angels,
Mighty in strength, who perform His word,
Obeying the voice of His word!
21
Bless the Lord, all you His angels,
You who serve Him, doing His will.
22
Bless the Lord, all you works of His,
In all places of His dominion;
Bless the Lord, my soul!

READ PSALM 103.

Compose your own similar psalm, using these prompts to guide you.

CALL on your inner self to praise God:

-
-
-
-
-
-
-

LIST WHAT GOD has done and continues to do for you:

-
-
-
-
-
-
-
-

WHAT ARE the characteristics of God?

-
-
-
-
-
-
-

HOW DOES God show who He is in how He deals with you?

-
-
-
-
-
-
-

REPEAT YOUR PRAISE:

-
-
-
-
-
-
-

ABOUT THE AUTHOR

Kirsten Panachyda and her husband Dan have two young adult sons, and together they are a roller-coaster-riding, travel-loving, blue-hair-dying family. They love Jesus and each other, but there is still a certain amount of sarcasm and sass. Kirsten is a speaker, Bible teacher, and award-winning writer. Softened by the experience of parenting a son with mental illness, she longs to extend compassion and infuse courage into the soul-weary. She loves to connect through her blog and website (Kirstenp.com) on Facebook (Kirsten Panachyda- Writer and Speaker), and Instagram (@kpanachyda).

Sign up to receive Kirsten's newsletter and receive the FREE RESOURCE Seven Days of Prayer for a Hurting Child at Kirstenp.com.

ALSO BY KIRSTEN PANACHYDA

Coming May 2021

Among Lions: Fighting for Faith and Finding your Rest while Parenting a
Child with Mental Illness

www.ingramcontent.com/pod-product-compliance
Lightning Source LLC
Chambersburg PA
CBHW060533030426
42337CB00021B/4236